You, Your Dog and THE LAW.

A dog owner's guide

by
Laceyn Thorpe LLB. (Hons)
Artwork by Antonella Ruscitto

ISBN 978-0-557-09662-6

Toffee

Dedication

This book is lovingly dedicated to man's best friend and to the staff and volunteers of all animal welfare organisations.

Let the world be a safer place for all our animal friends.
e&oe

This publication is a guide only, always consult a qualified solicitor.

Tiffanee

Contents

Hi mum.

Chapter 1

You and Your Puppy

You have been to your local breeder, selected your puppy and are about to go home. You have your receipt and his pedigree papers in your hand. Legally this dog is now your responsibility. He should be healthy and happy so take him to the vet for an initial health check and get him registered. The vet will then advise you of the date for his injections. It also gives you peace of mind that the puppy you have just bought is healthy and free of disease or defects. Is it a legislative requirement that you do this?

Strictly speaking, yes it is. You are legally obliged to take care of the puppy in a way that is responsible and not cruel. Failing to adequately look after the health and welfare of this puppy is contrary to the **Animal Welfare Act 2006 s.4**.

This section of the **2006 Act** deals with prevention of harm to dogs.

It says that an offence is committed if there is an act OR a failure to act to prevent harm to the animal. This section also states that the offence is committed if the person knew or should have known that the act or failure to act caused the suffering.

It is well known that dogs have injections to protect them from certain diseases and the breeder should have told you if the injections or part of the course have already been administered.

S.9 of the **2006 Act** further endorses this. It specifies the responsibilities of the owner in respect of diet, where it is housed, health, the ability of the dog to express its natural instinct and any need to be housed with or away from other animals. This latter point is significant because your puppy needs to be kept away from other dogs until his course of injections have taken affect. You should also get him micro-chipped so that in the event of loss or theft he can be identified and returned to you.

It is important to be aware of the law regarding the identification of your new charge when in a public place. This is governed by the **Control of Dogs Order 1992.**

The order states that any dog in a public place must wear a collar with the name and address including the postcode of the owner clearly engraved or written on it, or engraved on a tag. Your telephone number is not a requirement by law, but it is advisable.

There are exceptions to the rule, these are:
Dogs used on official duties by the armed forces, HM Customs & Excise or the police
Dogs used for sporting purposes and packs of hounds
Dogs used for the capture or destruction of vermin
Dogs used for driving or tending cattle or sheep
Guide Dogs for the Blind
Dogs used for emergency rescue work

It is also helpful to be aware that a breeder cannot sell a puppy under the age of 8 weeks pursuant to the **Breeding and Sale of Dogs (Welfare) Act 1999 s.8(1)(c).**

(At this stage it should be pointed out that the breeding of dogs and kennel ownership will be dealt with in a later chapter.)

Just because your puppy cannot socialise with other dogs at this time, does not mean he does not want to play. He needs a secure and safe area to play in. You have a legal duty to ensure his play area is safe and secure and most of all **escape proof**. If he gets out or into the neighbour's garden and digs up the flowers, **YOU** are liable for any loss or damage.

Mmmmmmm very tempting.

At common law your neighbours are entitled to the quiet enjoyment of their property, free from playful puppies digging up the lawn or chewing holes in the hosepipe. It may seem cute and funny but when the damage is potentially expensive and dangerous your puppy is suddenly not so cute any more and becomes a liability.

(Nuisance will be dealt with in a later chapter.)

The law does not recognise that because the puppy is so young he didn't know any better and that there is no liability on the owner. The liability for the dog owner starts from day one.

The other issue worthy of a mention here is **Occupiers' Liability**. Ensure everyone you invite into your home is made aware that you have a new dog. Not everyone likes dogs!

The Occupiers' Liability Act 1957 and the **Occupiers' Liability Act 1984**, governs the liability of owners and occupiers of all types of buildings and land to visitors, authorised or otherwise.

The **1984 Act** imposes a duty on an occupier where
(1) the state of the premises poses a danger and

(2) the danger is one that poses a risk of causing injury to a trespasser (it is convenient, though not

always accurate, to describe the 'non visitor') if he comes into the vicinity of the danger and

(3) there are reasonable grounds for believing that the trespasser is or may come into the vicinity of the danger and

(4) in all the circumstances of the case it is reasonable to afford the trespasser some protection against the risk.

*"If the plaintiff was a visitor..... the defendant would have owed a common duty of care under the **1957 Act**. This duty is to take such care as in all the circumstances is reasonable to see that she would be reasonably safe in using the premises for the purpose for which she was entitled to be there".* [1]

What does the law say about this?

If you invite someone into your home and they fall over the dog you are liable for any personal injury or loss. There is an exception though. If you invite someone into your lounge and when you go and make a cup of tea they wander off to look around the bedrooms without your permission and fall over the

---

[1]Burke v Southern Education and Library Board & Ors [2004] NIQB 13 at 33

dog half way up the stairs you have a defence of contributory negligence, likewise if you do not invite someone in and they wander into the house uninvited then the same rule applies. This is because they have entered areas of the property they do not have permission to be in.

Many people also buy signs saying things like "Beware of the dog".

Don't do it!

It implies that the dog is aggressive. Buy a sign that simply makes people aware there is a dog on the premises. Something simple such as "Dog on the premises." It simply states a fact and does not imply anything. Should something go wrong, it can be given in evidence that reasonable steps have been taken to make visitors aware that you have a dog. If you have a front garden then fix the sign firmly to the gate and ensure it is clearly visible. Do the same if there is a gate to the back garden. Understand that it does not reduce your liability but it shows that you have taken reasonable steps to make visitors aware of the presence of a dog.

Visitors have a duty of care to safeguard themselves too.

What happens if the vet has checked your puppy over and it is found that the animal is sick?
Your rights here are quite mixed. If you bought the pup from an unregistered breeder then it really is a case of "buyer beware". You can return the pup but your chances of a refund are negligible. In such a case you should report the breeder to the **Royal Society for the Prevention of Cruelty to Animals (RSPCA)**. The RSPCA has the power to seize animals that are maltreated and bring prosecutions against offenders. (See useful addresses section at the back of the book.)

If the breeder is registered you will usually find that they will co-operate as it could damage their business severely if it is found that sick animals are being sold. It does happen but it is thankfully rare.

The legalities in this instance will be dealt with in a later chapter.

Let me out of here.

Conclusion

- You have a legal duty of care to the dog and the public from day one.

- Ensure your dog has a collar and identity tag.

- Ensure the dog sees a vet to have him registered, checked over and arrange for him to have his injections if required.

- Ensure the dog has a safe, secure, escape proof play area.

- Make sure the dog is given the attention he needs. At this early stage NEVER leave him alone in your home get a puppy sitter if you need to go out and leave the dog home.

- Make sure your friends know you have a new dog and put up signs informing people of his presence.

Don't touch my bone!

Chapter 2

He's Growing Up

The teething is over and being a responsible owner you take your dog out regularly and he goes to training classes. He is well natured and good with other dogs. What could possibly go wrong?

In law, it only takes one slip up for you to end up before the courts. The major issues in recent times involve dangerous dogs, nuisance dogs, dog fouling of the public highway and public spaces.

Clearing up after your dog
To many people this is an unpleasant chore but it is a necessary one, the **Dogs (Fouling of Land) Act 1996** makes this a legal requirement in most areas.

What does this mean to you?
If you generally take it that you must clean up after your dog in any place to which the public has access even if the land is privately owned then you cannot go far wrong. Most public parks have bins to dispose of dog faeces so if you run your dog in the park take some bags with you to pick it up. This is not always possible if the dog faeces are runny so take a bottle of water with you to break it down and disperse it.

As long as an effort is made to do this then in the eyes of the law you have taken the reasonable steps required for cleaning up after your dog. The **Clean Neighbourhoods and Environment Act 2005** gives local authorities the power to fine offenders up to **£1000** for failure to do this.

The **Road Traffic Act 1988** makes it an offence to have a dog on a designated road without the dog being held on a lead. The **Clean Neighbourhoods and Environment Act 2005** also allows local authorities to designate areas of land where dogs must be kept on leads, or where dogs are excluded and also places limits on the number of dogs walked by a single person. This varies depending on where you live so check with your local council.

Is your dog a nuisance?
Nuisance in law is divided into two areas, public nuisance and private nuisance. It covers a multitude of sins from noisy neighbours playing loud music to corporate organisations creating nasty odours from their working processes.

No matter how well trained your dog is he can still become a nuisance.

Public nuisance is generally accepted as anything that happens in the street or a public place that affects a class of person or persons. Public nuisance is a crime and is something that materially interferes with the reasonable comfort and convenience of the class of person or persons.

To translate this into English, imagine you have tied your dog up to go into a shop and your dog growls and barks at anyone who tries to enter or leave the shop while you are in there. This comes under the remit of **The Dangerous Dogs Act 1991 s.3. Keeping dogs under control,** and **s.7(1)(a) and (b) Muzzling and Leads.**

This is a public nuisance. The class of person or persons are those who wish to use or leave the shop. The offence is that having tied the dog up and left him, the dog is not under control. The comfort and convenience is the fact that people want to enter or leave the shop without fear or interference. This is a general overview of the law however what if the dog bites someone in your garden?

In **Bogdal v R**[1], Mr Bogdal owned a German shepherd dog that was tied up on his land. He previously owned the land and building next to his own land but had sold it and the building on it became a private nursing home

---

[1] **[2008] EWCA Crim 1**

Three people were bitten by the dog whilst walking or riding a bicycle up the drive. Mr Bogdal was convicted under the **Dangerous Dogs Act 1991. s.10**

Mr Bogdal appealed against his conviction and won on the grounds that the drive was a private road and not a public highway.

The issue in this case was if the land where the offence took place was private or public? In this case their Lordships took the view that the driveway was private and Mr Bogdal was cleared of the offences he was charged with, namely having a dog out of control in a public place.

In **Fellowes v Director of Public Prosecutions**[2]

The complainant was a schoolboy delivering a newspaper to a maisonette. He was attacked by the defendant's dog while he was on the path which led through from the defendant's front gate to his front door. The path only served that particular dwelling and ran through an area of which the defendant had the exclusive use.

It was argued for the Crown that the path was a "public place" because members of the public who had lawful business with the occupier had an implied invitation to use it in order to reach the front door.

---

[2] Briefly reported in The Times for 1.2.93

The Court rejected that submission. It relied on two earlier decisions in cases concerned with the definition of "public place" in other statutes.

Both these cases show a clear defence, however the last thing you want is to be brought before the courts as you may not be quite so fortunate.

The judge in **Bogdal** said in his closing statement:

"However, we wish in conclusion strongly to encourage Mr and Mrs Bogdal to take steps (if they have not already done so) to ensure that there is no repetition of the incidents which gave rise to the prosecution and that the dog in question does not pose a risk to legitimate users of the driveway serving Wawne House and Sycamore House. The fact that that driveway is not a public place does not mean that they may not incur civil liabilities arising out of its behaviour or get into trouble with the law in other ways than under the 1991 Act."

Private nuisance is where there is an interference with the quiet enjoyment and/or use of land, some right over it or in connection with it. The classic example here is the barking dog. Nothing will annoy your neighbours more than your dog continually barking night and day. This is generally one of the most common complaints against dog owners.

Remember! It is in your dog's nature to protect you and your home, hence he will bark. He will also do this if he feels threatened in any way or feels he needs your attention.

Within the sphere of private nuisance we also have **nuisance to servitudes**. This includes an example where different people share pathways, drives and private roads that serve more than one property.

If you own a piece of land that your neighbour(s) have a right to cross for access to their homes but your dog prevents them from walking across the land because they are frightened of dogs or the dog barks or growls at them, then the dog could be classed as a nuisance. This is because the rights of the neighbour are being interfered with even though the dog is on his home property. This also applies to people who have a right to walk on your property like policemen, postmen other emergency services and utilities workers who have **statutory rights** to perform certain functions and require access either to your property or need to cross your land to perform their lawful duty.

This is where signs stating you own a dog is helpful. You are alerting these people to the fact that you have a dog on the premises. This does not release you from any subsequent liability but may help to mitigate an incident. The legal term **Volenti Non Fit Injuria** meaning **contributory negligence** may come into play. If the person with the right of way walks across your land knowing that the dog is there then you might be able to mitigate any problems but you cannot rely on this defence completely although you should note the judge's comments above.

Do you have a dangerous dog?

It is certainly an indictment on our society that certain people gain enjoyment from watching dogs fight, often to the death. It is something that has happened for centuries but at long last the law in England and Wales recognises this evil practice as being serious enough to make it illegal.

Unfortunately, certain breeds of dog have been bred specifically for this purpose.
The **Dangerous Dogs Act 1991 (DDA) s.1(2)** states that it is illegal to own, breed, offer for sale, advertise for sale, exchange, make a gift of, or import certain breeds of dog.

Under **s.1 of the 1991 Act** these are:

1(a) Pitbull Terrier
1(b) Japanese Tosa

Included on the list are the Dogo Argentino and the Fila Braziliero.

The above offences under the **DDA 1991** carry, upon conviction, a **fine of up to £5000 or six months imprisonment or both.**

The **Town Police Clauses Act 1847** (outside London) and the **Metropolitan Police Act 1839** (London) make it an offence to allow an unmuzzled, ferocious dog to be left at large, or for a person to set on or to urge any dog attack, worry or put in fear any person or animal in the street.

In addition to the statutory liability, there also remains the common law remedy under the **scienter**[3] action and the liability in negligence [4] or in trespass (if the owner has commanded the dog to attack).

---

[3] Scienter action is where the owner knew or should have known of the dog's propensity to attack visitors.
[4] *Kavanagh v. Stokes* [1942] I.R. 596

Damage caused in an attack on a person need not involve physical contact – the word 'attack' though not defined (in this Act) has been judicially defined as including an assault which does not, necessarily, involve battery. Indeed, in the commentary to this section **Kerr, Irish Current Law Statutes Annotated at 86/32-44** suggests that "physical contact may arise where a person falls and injures themselves when getting out of the way of an attacking dog[5]."

Young Persons

What happens if the owner of the dog or the person having the care and control is under the age of 16 years old?

The law is clear on this issue The **DDA s.6** states that if the owner of a dog is under 16 years old, the responsibility for the dog reverts to the head of the household. This is the parent, guardian or person with legal responsibility for the young person.

---

[5]Quinlisk v. Kearney & Ors [2004] IEHC 96

It is very important to understand that a police officer or dog warden can seize any dog that falls within the remit of a dangerous dog or any dog that is dangerously out of control.

I try to look as mean as possible.

Conclusion

- Remember that certain breeds of dog are illegal to own in the United Kingdom.

- It is illegal to attend; stage or provide dogs for the purposes of dog fighting.

- Keep your dog under control at all times[6], even on your own property.

- Never use your dog as a weapon or to threaten anyone or anything.

- Only a person over the age of 16 can take full responsibility for a dog
- The police or a dog warden may seize any dog that is dangerous or out of control.

---

[6] Briscoe v Shattock [1998] EWHC Admin 929

Mum Dad, I can walk myself.

Chapter Three

Out and About

Your dog and the countryside.
Most dogs love a good run and the chance to play in the countryside on a sunny summers' day. As a responsible dog owner you must remember that livestock do not make good playmates for your dog. If your dog was born, bred and raised in an urban environment he will probably have never seen a sheep, a cow or a horse. Some breeds of dog have a natural inclination to herd animals and sometimes people. It may have been in their breeding for generations. Breeds such as German Shepherds and Collies are typical examples. They also have an instinct to hunt. What may appear to be a desire by your dog to play can quickly turn into something very different.

What does the law mention about this?
Initially reference to the **Dangerous Dogs Act 1991,** as mentioned in **chapter 2** above, are applicable to this issue however there are further legal issues that are important in this context.

Sheep worrying was brought to the fore some years ago, although it is not as prominent in the press as it used to be it is still a big issue for farmers. A marked number of sheep and lambs are lost every year due to dog worrying, this is not just through direct attack but also through miscarriage of lambs caused by stress and fear.

This is not acceptable even through accidental means.

There are ranges of offences that can be committed by your dog being allowed to do this.

You can also be charged with criminal damage. This is because the **Criminal Damage Act 1971 s.10 (a)** *includes wild creatures, which have been tamed or are ordinarily kept in captivity. (Sheep, cows, horses, chickens etc.)*

The **Animals Act 1971** gives a farmer certain rights. The farmer has the right to stop your dog from worrying his livestock on agricultural land and he may shoot your dog without warning under certain circumstances so keep your dog under control at all times.

You could face criminal prosecution for the same offence under the **Dogs (Protection of Livestock) Act 1953.** As well as a fine, a term of imprisonment or both your dog could be seized and/or destroyed.

Poaching

Within this context, dogs are also used for poaching. **The Night Poaching Act 1828 s.1** *makes it an offence for a person to take, destroy or enter land for the purpose of poaching game or rabbits by night. 'Game includes pheasants and grouse and the like.* Night is deemed under **s.12 of the 1828 Act** *to be at the expiration of 1 hour after sunset.*

The **Game Act 1831** is worded in a similar way to the **Night Poaching Act 1828** except it refers to the daytime. *For the purposes of this Act 'daytime is deemed to commence at the beginning of the last hour before sunrise.* **The Deer Act 1991** works in a similar way.

The basic message is **Do not poach!** It is a criminal offence.

Hunting with Dogs

Different people have different views on hunting with dogs. Some think it is reprehensible and others think it is a good way of keeping the numbers of foxes and other wild animals under control. After a lengthy debate with arguments for and against hunting with dogs, parliament finally passed the following legislation.

The **Hunting Act 2004** effectively bans the hunting of all wild animals with dogs. This also includes hare coursing.

S.1 of the Act clearly states:
"A person commits an offence if he hunts a wild mammal with a dog, unless his hunting is exempt."

The wording is clear and needs no real explanation, but what is "exempt"?

In law this simply means there are some exceptions to the rule.

S.2 of the **2004 Act** allows for these exceptions.
Exempt hunting
Hunting is exempt if it is within a class specified in
Schedule 1 of the 2004 Act.
- **Stalking and flushing out**
- **Use of dogs below ground to protect birds for shooting**
- **Rats**

- **Rabbits**
- **Retrieval of hares**
- **Falconry**
- **Recapture of wild mammal**
- **Rescue of a wild mammal**
- **Research and observation**

Stalking a wild mammal, or flushing it out of cover, is exempt hunting if certain conditions are satisfied.

Stalking or flushing out is undertaken for the purpose of preventing or reducing serious damage which the wild mammal would otherwise cause to livestock, to game birds or wild birds, food for livestock, crops, growing timber, fisheries, other property or to the biological diversity[1] of an area for the purposes of obtaining meat to be used for human or animal consumption or for participation in a field trial.

The term, "field trial" means a competition (other than a hare coursing event in which dogs Flush animals out of cover or retrieves animals that have been shot (or both), and are assessed as to their likely usefulness in connection with shooting.

---

[1] Within the meaning of the United Nations Environmental Programme Convention on Biological Diversity of 1992).

Stalking or flushing out takes place on land which belongs to the person doing the stalking or flushing out, or which he has been given permission to use for the purpose by the occupier or, in the case of unoccupied land, by a person to whom it belongs and does not involve the use of more than two dogs and does not involve the use of a dog below ground.

The use of a dog below ground in the course of stalking or flushing out is permitted if the following conditions are met.
The stalking or flushing out is undertaken for the purpose of preventing or reducing serious damage to game birds or wild birds[2] which a person is keeping or preserving for the purpose of their being shot.

The person doing the stalking or flushing out which a person is keeping or preserving for the purpose of their being shot has with him written evidence that the land on which the stalking or flushing out takes place belongs to him, or that he has been given permission to use that land for the purpose by the occupier or, in the case of unoccupied land, by a person to whom it belongs, and makes the evidence

---

[2] Within the meaning of section 27 of the Wildlife and Countryside Act 1981 as amended (England and Wales) (Amendment) Regulations 2004 SI 2004/1487

immediately available for inspection by a constable who asks to see it.

It does not involve the use of more than one dog below ground at any one time.
The fifth condition is that reasonable steps are taken for the purpose of ensuring that as soon as possible after being found or flushed out the wild mammal is shot dead by a competent person, and in particular, each dog used in the stalking or flushing out is kept under sufficiently close control to ensure that it does not prevent or obstruct achievement of the objective in the above paragraph.

The hunting of rats is exempt if it takes place on land which belongs to the hunter, or which he has been given permission to use for the purpose by the occupier or, in the case of unoccupied land, by a person to whom it belongs.

The hunting of rabbits is exempt if it takes place on land- (a) which belongs to the hunter, or (b) which he has been given permission to use for the purpose by the occupier or, in the case of unoccupied land, by a person to whom it belongs.

The hunting of a hare which has been shot is exempt if it takes place on land which belongs to the hunter, or which he has been given permission to use for the purpose of hunting hares by the occupier or, in the case of unoccupied land, by a person to whom it belongs.

Flushing a wild mammal from cover is exempt hunting if undertaken for the purpose of enabling a bird of prey to hunt the wild mammal, and on land which belongs to the hunter or which he has been given permission to use for the purpose by the occupier or, in the case of unoccupied land, by a person to whom it belongs.
The hunting of a wild mammal which has escaped or been released from captivity or confinement is exempt if the following conditions are satisfied.

The hunting takes place on land that belongs to the hunter, on land that he has been given permission to use for the purpose by the occupier or, in the case of unoccupied land, by a person to whom it belongs, or with the authority of a constable.

Also reasonable steps are taken for the purpose of ensuring that as soon as possible after being found the wild mammal is recaptured or shot dead by a competent person, and in particular, each dog used in the hunt is kept under sufficiently close control to ensure that it does not prevent or obstruct achievement of dispatching or capturing the animal. The wild mammal must not have been released for the purpose of being hunted, and was not, for that purpose, permitted to escape.

The hunting of a wild mammal for the purposes of rescuing it is exempt if the following conditions are satisfied.

The hunter reasonably believes that the wild mammal is or may be injured.

The hunting is undertaken for the purpose of relieving the wild mammal's suffering.

The hunting does not involve the use of more than two dogs and does not involve the use of a dog below ground.

The hunting takes place on land that belongs to the hunter, on land that he has been given permission to use for the purpose by the occupier or, in the case of unoccupied land, by a person to whom it belongs, or with the authority of a constable.

Also, reasonable steps are taken for the purpose of ensuring that as soon as possible after the wild mammal is found appropriate action (if any) is taken to relieve its suffering, and in particular, each dog used in the hunt is kept under sufficiently close control to ensure that it does not prevent or obstruct any action taken in the best interest of the wild mammal and the wild mammal was not harmed for the purpose of enabling it to be hunted.

The hunting of a wild mammal is exempt if it is undertaken for the purpose of or in connection with the observation or study of the wild mammal and that the hunting does not involve the use of more than two dogs.

The hunting does not involve the use of a dog below ground and the hunting takes place on land which belongs to the hunter, or which he has been given permission to use for the purpose by the occupier or, in the case of unoccupied land, by a person to whom it belongs and that each dog used in the hunt is kept under sufficiently close control to ensure that it does not injure the wild mammal.

Wildlife and Countryside Act 1981 (c. 69) (As amended) Section 27

This section defines what, in law, constitutes a wild animal or wild bird.

"Wild animal" *means any animal (other than a bird) which is or (before it was killed or taken) was living wild;*

"Wild bird" *means any bird of a kind which is ordinarily resident in or is a visitor to Great Britain in a wild state but does not include poultry or, except in **sections 5** and **16**, any game bird;*

Conclusion

- When out and about keep your dog under control and on a lead at all times.

- Do not poach, it is illegal.

- Do not hunt foxes with hounds. It is illegal.

- Note the exempt hunting activities and be mindful of the requirements.

I feel sick.

Chapter 4

Feeling Poorly

Dogs, just like people, sometimes become ill or have accidents. When this happens it means a trip to the vet. It is vital to understand at this point that you **must not** under any circumstances attempt to treat your dog yourself, you may be committing an offence under the **Veterinary Surgeons Act 1966 section 19.**

To recap briefly, it has already been mentioned in **chapter one** about your responsibility and duty of care to your dog. I see no point in repeating it again here except to remind you about causing unnecessary suffering to your dog. If you fail to take your dog to the vet if he is ill or injured you may be guilty of an offence by omission. That is to say you did not do something when you should have. In law, you can be as guilty of failing to do something as you are if you do something wrong. This is because your failure to do something such as failing to take the dog to the vet when he is sick may cause unnecessary suffering.

The vet

Your vet is a very highly trained medical practitioner who works with animals and birds of all varieties, although your vet will specialize in a particular type of animal. Horses for example, he/she will be perfectly qualified to treat your dog. The vet will have studied a recognized course of veterinary medicine at a duly credited university or higher education establishment described by the **1966 Act**.

The course of study will have been accredited by the Royal College of Veterinary Surgeons (RCVS), who also regulate and police the profession. Vets are governed by the **Veterinary Surgeons Act 1966** and disciplinary proceedings are very formal

Just like doctors in hospitals, a vet can be struck off the register and be stopped from working as a vet for mal-practice and/or misconduct[1]. The trend has been more to suspend a vet rather than stop him working[2]

It should be noted that medical negligence of any kind is notoriously difficult to prove and any

---

[1]Under ss.15/16 of the Veterinary Surgeons Act 1966.
[2] Walker v. The Royal College of Veterinary Surgeons(RCVS) (21 November 2007) [2007] UKPC 64 (21 November 2007)

proceedings against a vet can be very costly and the outcome very uncertain. It does, however, retain the advantage of having a lower burden of proof. The judgment is made on a balance of probabilities, not the reasonable doubt required by criminal proceedings in the magistrates and crown courts.

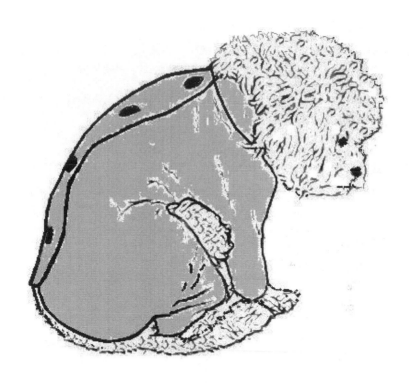

Does the vet make house calls?

Prescriptions

The **Misuse of Drugs Act 1971** permits a qualified vet to administer and prescribe medicines for animals. You should note that not all veterinary surgeries carry enough stock to issue medicines "over the counter", or may not be licensed for this. Always check for this eventuality. If your vet prescribes a medical treatment for your dog, you are not obliged to purchase it from that vet, you have the right to "shop around" and fill the prescription from any officially recognised source such as a dispensing chemist.

As with all official bodies there is a complaints procedure that can be followed. The **RCVS** can be contacted easily by phone or email. (See the Useful Contacts page at the end of this book.)

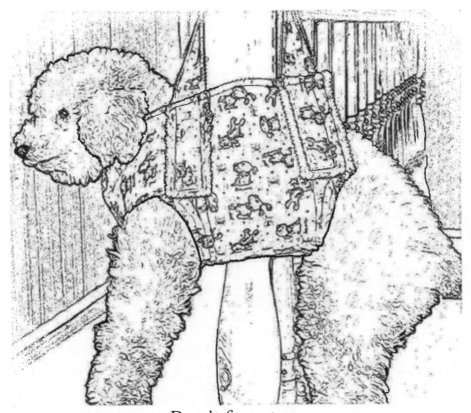

Don't forget me.

Chapter 5

On Vacation

Holidays can possibly have legal implications. This really has more to do with going abroad on holidays.

Different countries have different rules regarding the import and export of dogs. As far as England and Wales is concerned it is possible to have a **"pet passport"**. If you wish, for example to go to an EU member state for a month, you may use a pet passport. This document tells the authorities that your dog is fully inoculated against infectious diseases and is free of rabies. You need to note that your dog needs to be checked by a qualified, registered vet in your foreign destination prior to your return to the UK.

Failure to comply with the regulations will mean a six-month stay in a quarantine kennels for your dog. **Regulation (EC) No 998/2003 amending Council Directive 92/65/EEC.** Your dog must also be easily identifiable. **Under Art 4 para 1 (a) and (b).** Your dog must either be clearly tattooed (a) or microchipped with a readable transducer (b). The dog must also travel by an approved route.

For countries without an approved route it is expected for your dog to be licensed into quarantine with a view to obtaining early release. A list of countries to which the Pet Travel Scheme applies covers more than just EU member countries. The EU published a full list of countries and is available on the web via the EU official website It is also available as a link from the **Department for Environment, Food, Rural Affairs and Agriculture. (Defra)** official Website.

Carriage of dogs on aircraft.
Dogs cannot be carried in the passenger area of a commercial aircraft. All animals are shipped in crates in the hold of the aircraft. Defra will be able to advise you of the size and design of a suitable carrier for your dog. They also have a list of approved carriers and freight forwarders for this purpose.

The regulations governing carriage of freight by air are very strict and leave very little room for flexibility so it is important to get it right first time. Mistakes can be costly and your dog may be refused permission to travel.

Mmmm! I love Pina Colladas!

Conclusion

- It is possible to take your dog abroad and bring him back without having to quarantine him.
- Make sure all the paperwork is correct prior to travel.
- Ensure you have the correct crate for your dog to be transported in.

- Make your arrangements well before you plan to travel. (7 months is a good period)

- It is important that you contact your local Animal Health Divisional Office (AHDO) or the authorities (e.g. the Embassy) and check the requirements.

- For animals travelling abroad on the PETS scheme and intending to return to the UK there is a 6 month interval after a successful blood test before your pet can re-enter the UK.

- A small proportion of animals will fail to reach the required blood antibody levels. In this case, you will need to pay for a second rabies vaccination and blood sample.

- After the first or rabies vaccination, it is not possible to enter another EU country for at least 21 days after the date of the vaccination. However, this can vary.

- Dogs and cats being exported to countries outside of the PETS travel scheme will have different requirements for rabies vaccination and in some cases tests to exclude other diseases.

- If your pet remains in another country for more than a few weeks it may become subject to that country's rules of residence.

- Some countries do not allow certain types of dogs to enter (dangerous breeds) and may have special rules on others.

- Microchip - it is important to check that your pet's microchip is working before travelling

How do I look?

Chapter 6

Working Dogs

It is always a delight to see working dog displays at various shows and functions; these are often displays by police dogs or dogs from the armed services. The handlers as well as the dogs are very highly trained. Not all make the grade for different reasons.

Some civilian security companies provide dog and handler services to guard premises. The law is very specific if your dog is used as a guard dog in this way.

There are three key things to remember under the **Guard Dogs Act 1975**.

The dog must be under the control of a handler at all times.

The dog must not be allowed to roam free (off the lead).

There must be signs clearly displayed warning the public that guard dogs are used on the premises. (Usually on entry and exit gates and external fences.)

It is also important to remember that the dog in this context is no more than a deterrent. **HE IS NOT A WEAPON!** You must inform an intruder to leave the premises; you must give them a reasonable time to do so. Should they fail to do so you have the right to use **REASONABLE** force to remove them.

If you have reason to believe that offences have been committed or are going to be committed you must inform the police. Although laws exist stating you can make a citizen's arrest it is not recommended. Let the police do their job.

You will often find that if intruders see a dog they will run or not enter the premises in the first place. If they run just inform the police. **DO NOT** let the dog go after them. You may be committing an offence, although in saying that there have been cases where a police dog has bitten someone other than the target suspect without redress to the law[1].

---

[1]Gloster v Greater Manchester Police [2000] EWCA Civ 90

There are a number of cases where trained police dogs have bitten someone they should not have. In **Livesey v Chief Constable of Lancashire** an off duty police officer was bitten by a police dog whilst exercising it in a park. There was no liability in this case either. The claims had been made under **s.2 of the Animals Act 1971.** This section of the **1971 Act** has left their Lordships in a state of confusion over how to interpret paragraph **2(2) (b).** In **Cummings v Granger**[2], their Lordships stated that:

"A trained or conditioned guard dog will never come within section 2(2) (b) of the Act of 1971".

(2)(b) of the **Act of 1971".**
S.2 of the **1971 Act** *provides, insofar as is material:*
"(1) Where any damage is caused by an animal which belongs to a dangerous species, any person who is a keeper of the animal is liable for the damage, except as otherwise provided by this Act.
(2) Where damage is caused by an animal which does not belong to a dangerous species, a keeper of the animal is liable for the damage, except as otherwise provided by this Act, if—

---

[2] Cummings v Granger [1977] QB 397 at 400

When we're not at work, he doesn't have to call me boss and I'll even share my bone with him.

(a) the damage is of a kind which the animal, unless restrained, was likely to cause or which, if caused by the animal, was likely to be severe; and
(b) the likelihood of the damage or of its being severe was due to characteristics of the animal which are not normally found in animals of the same species or are not normally so found except at particular times or in particular circumstances;
(c) those characteristics are known to that keeper.."

As a security guard you are a civilian, not a police officer. The rules governing the use of dogs to restrain or detain suspects are different from police and military personnel. Often civilian security staff uses their own untrained dogs and rely on the dog's natural sense to protect its master and territory.

*In **Cummings v Granger** above, and **Curtis v Betts**[3] the so-called second limb in s.2(2)(b) was relied on. In neither case did the dog, an **Alsatian** in **Cummings** and a **bull mastiff** in **Curtis**, have characteristics not normally found in such dogs but they did display such characteristics in the "particular circumstances" present in those cases; an untrained dog roaming a yard which it regarded as its territory and a dog with a tendency to react fiercely when defending what he regarded as his own territory.*

Dogs can have different jobs apart from guarding. Some dogs perform tricks for the enjoyment of crowds. Others have a life devoted to helping people such as search and rescue, Guide dogs for the blind, Hearing dogs for the deaf and hard of hearing, Companion dogs for the ill and infirm.

---

[3] Curtis v Betts [1990] 1 WLR 459

Conclusion

- Always keep your dog under control and on a lead when he is working unless it is reasonably impractical to do so or it may cause unnecessary injury or distress to the dog or a member of the public.

- Gun dogs such as spaniels and Labrador retrievers used to retrieve game birds cannot work on leads.

- Dogs used to herd sheep do not work on a lead.

- Alternatively guide dogs always work in a harness.

- Dogs in competitions such as obedience and field trials will be worked both on and off the lead. The law provides for these exceptions.

I should be cloned

Chapter 7

Breeding Dogs and Kennel Ownership

There is much to be said about people who breed dogs. Some do it for profit, some do it improve the breed, some do it because they think it is good for a bitch to have at least one litter, others end up with a litter after an "accident".

So you've shown your dog a few times and won a few rosettes and everyone tells you what a beautiful dog you have and that you should use your dog for breeding purposes.

(The Kennel Club has a web site with a wealth of information about responsible dog breeding, showing and breed standards. See the useful addresses section at the end of the book.)

You think it's a great idea and decide to have a litter. So-far so-good, nothing illegal there. You have done your research and found a sire. You've read every book on your breed in the library and spoken to every breeder you know.

You wait for the right time and you mate your dog, then whoopeeeeee! Sixty-three days later you have six cute little puppies……. And hey, you still havn't broken the law.

UNLESS the vet advised you not to breed from your bitch or she was very young, this is very irresponsible and dangerous for the dog. In legal terms it means you were reckless as to the health and welfare of your dog, thus endangering her.

This is an offence because you will have caused her unnecessary distress and/or harm. Whelping is a stressful time for a bitch under the best of conditions. If she is not at her best you could loose her and your puppies.

You must be mindful of the 2006 Act at all times.

So you set up a whelping area, all the puppies and mum are doing well. The word has got out and people start phoning you to buy a puppy.

It is advisable to tell your prospective buyers when they will be ready for collection, remember, **it is an offence to sell a puppy under the age of 8 weeks.**

If you have a breed of dog that traditionally has its tail docked beware! It is now illegal to dock tails unless certain criteria are met.

Basically a dog's tail can only be docked by a qualified vet for the following reasons:-

- The docking is for medical reasons.
- It is necessary because of the nature of the work the dog does.
- The owner must show evidence that the dog is a working dog.

In **England**, the following breeds may be docked:

- Hunt point retrieve breeds of any type or combination of types
- Spaniels of any type or combination of types
- Terriers of any type or combination of types

In **Wales**, the following breeds may be docked:-

- Spaniels of the following breeds; English Springer; Welsh Springer and Cocker, but not combinations of the breeds

- Terriers of the following breeds; Jack Russell, Cairn, Lakeland, Norfolk, but not combinations of the breed.
- Hunt point retrievers of the following breeds; Braque Italian, Brittany, German Long Haired Pointer, German Short Haired Pointer, German Wire Haired Pointer, Hungarian Vizsla, Hungarian Wire Haired Vizsla, Italian Spinone, Spanish Water Dog, Weimaraner, Korthals Griffon, Slovakian Rough Haired Pointer, Large Musterlander, Small Musterlander.

Note The vet will always have the final decision to dock or not.

So the puppies leave you at 10 weeks old and they have all gone to good homes. You sold them for a handsome fee less the fee for the sire (unless you own him as well) and everyone is happy.

You pop off to the vet with your dog and have her checked over. She is given a clean bill of health so you decide to open a kennels.

You have a bank account full of money and you dash off and buy a kennelling property. You have space to breed, board paying customers and a facility for quarantine, all kindly set up by the previous owner who stopped dog activity some years before. You have a clean slate.

I shall not be discussing conveyancing of the property or planning permission as this is not what this book is about. We shall assume that everything went smoothly.

Welcome to the legalities of the breeding, boarding and quarantine kennels.

We met at a Christmas party.

Breeding Dogs

Let us assume you have a stock of 10 bitches and 6 dogs to be used for breeding purposes. You now require a breeding licence. **Breeding of Dogs Act 1973 ("the 1973 Act")**, is the first piece of legislation we will look at.

S.4A of the 1973 Act sets out the definition of Breeding establishments for dogs.

First of all you make your application for a license to your local authority, they will then send out an inspector and a vet to talk to you and inspect your premises. They then have three months from the date of the application to compile a report and your license is then given to you with any attached conditions.

Your license will last for 1 year from the date specified by you as the starting date on the application or by the date it was granted, whichever is the later.

*If you carry on a business of breeding dogs without a license you may be **imprisoned for up to 3 months, fined or both***.

Your license can be suspended if you are found to be breaking the law in some way. E.g. failure to keep accurate records.

Sale of dogs

(S.8 1973 Act)

(1) The keeper of a licensed breeding establishment is guilty of an offence if–

(a) he sells a dog otherwise than at a licensed breeding establishment, a licensed pet shop or a licensed Scottish rearing establishment,

(b) he sells a dog otherwise than to the keeper of a licensed pet shop or a licensed Scottish rearing establishment knowing or believing that the person who buys it intends that it should be sold (by him or any other person),

(c) he sells a dog which is less than eight weeks old otherwise than to the keeper of a licensed pet shop or a licensed Scottish rearing establishment,

(d) he sells to the keeper of a licensed pet shop or a licensed Scottish rearing establishment a dog which was not born at a licensed breeding establishment, or

(e) he sells to the keeper of a licensed pet shop or a licensed Scottish rearing establishment a dog which,

when delivered, is not wearing a collar with an identifying tag or badge.

*A person guilty of an offence under **s.8** is liable on summary conviction to a **fine, imprisonment or both.***

*Where a person is convicted of an offence under **s. 8(1) or (2)**, the court before which he/she is convicted may (in addition to or in substitution for any penalty under subsection (1)) make an order providing for any one or more of the following–*

*(a) the cancellation of any licence held by him under the **1973 Act**,*

*(b) his disqualification, for such period as the court thinks fit, from keeping an establishment the keeping of which is required to be licensed under the **1973 Act**, and*

(c) his disqualification, for such period as the court thinks fit, from having custody of any dog of a description specified in the order.

Boarding Kennels

This part of your kennels will be licensed in a similar way to the breeding side of the business and your license will state the maximum number of dogs you can board at any one time. It will also verify the conditions in which the dogs are kept and the precautions for the safety and the welfare of the dogs.

Licensing of boarding establishments for animals. Animal Boarding Establishments Act 1963. s.1 clearly states:

No person shall keep a boarding establishment for animals except under the authority of a licence granted in accordance with the provisions of this Act. **S.1 (3)** of the **1963 Act** establishes the criterion for the granting of a boarding license.

In determining whether to grant a licence for the keeping of a boarding establishment for animals by any person at any premises, a local authority shall in particular (but without prejudice to their discretion to withhold a licence on other grounds) have regard to the need for securing —
(a) that animals will at all times be kept in accommodation suitable as respects construction, size of quarters, number of occupants, exercising facilities, temperature, lighting, ventilation and cleanliness;

(b) that animals will be adequately supplied with suitable food, drink and bedding material, adequately exercised, and (so far as necessary) visited at suitable intervals;

(c) that all reasonable precautions will be taken to prevent and control the spread among animals of infectious or contagious diseases, including the provision of adequate isolation facilities;

(d) that appropriate steps will be taken for the protection of the animals in case of fire or other emergency;

*(e) that a register be kept containing a description of any animals received into the establishment, date of arrival and departure, and the name and address of the owner, such register to be available for inspection at all times by an officer of the local authority, veterinary surgeon or veterinary practitioner authorised under **section 2(1)** of this Act;*

*and shall specify such conditions in the licence, if granted by them, as appear to the local authority necessary or expedient in the particular case for securing all the objects specified in paragraphs **(a) to (e) of this subsection**.*

S.2(1) reads:
(1) A local authority may authorise in writing any of its officers or any veterinary surgeon or veterinary

practitioner to inspect (subject to compliance with such precautions as the authority may specify to prevent the spread among animals of infectious or contagious diseases) any premises in their area as respects which a licence granted in accordance with the provisions of this Act is for the time being in force, and any person authorised under this section may, on producing his authority if so required, enter any such premises at all reasonable times and inspect them and any animals found thereon or any thing therein, for the purpose of ascertaining whether an offence has been or is being committed against this Act.

(2) Any person who wilfully obstructs or delays any person in the exercise of his powers of entry or inspection under this section shall be guilty of an offence.

This simply means it is an offence to stop any authorised person from inspecting your kennels under this Act.

Quarantine Kennels

The United Kingdom is considered rabies free and the government intend to keep it that way. Unless a dog has a valid "pet passport", it is required, by law that a dog goes into quarantine for six months prior to release to its owner and into the public domain.

Release from quarantine
If a pet dog, cat or ferret is in quarantine in England, the Secretary of State may grant a licence releasing it if he/she is satisfied that -

(a) it has been identified and vaccinated (including any revaccination where required) in accordance with the requirements of **Regulation (EC) No. 998/2003 and the Non Commercial Movement of Pet Animals (England) Regulations 2004;**

(b) at least 24 hours before release it has been treated by a veterinary surgeon against Echinococcus multilocularis and ticks (and in the case of treatment against Echinococcus multilocularis the treatment contains praziquantel as the active ingredient);

(c) a neutralising antibody titration has been carried out on a blood sample from it in accordance with the requirements of **Regulation (EC) No. 998/2003 and the Non Commercial Movement of Pet Animals (England) Regulations 2004** *and the result is in accordance with the requirements of those instruments;*

*(d) the waiting period before entry to England required by **Regulation (EC) No. 998/2003 and the Non Commercial Movement of Pet Animals (England) Regulations 2004** has elapsed; and*

*(e) it has not been outside the countries and territories in **Annex II of Regulation (EC) No. 998/2003** in the **six months** prior to its import to England.".*

*This Order makes amendments to the **Rabies (Importation of Dogs, Cats and Other Mammals) Order 1974 (S.I. 1974/2211 as amended,** "the principal Order"). Most of the amendments are consequential on the application of **Regulation (EC) No. 998/2003 of the European Parliament and the Council of 26 May 2003** on the animal health requirements applicable to the non-commercial movement of pet animals and amending **Council Directive 92/65/EEC (OJ No. L146, 13.6.2003, p1), as amended by Commission Regulation (EC) No. 592/2004 (OJ No. L 94, 31.3.2004, p7) (The Community Regulation.")***

*The Community Regulation is administered and enforced by the **Non Commercial Movement of Pet Animals (England) Regulations 2004 ("the Non Commercial Movement Regulations"),** which revoke* and replace the **Pet Travel Scheme (Pilot Arrangements) (England) Order 1999** and come into force simultaneously with this Order.

The Order amends the principal Order consequentially to the Community Regulation to:

(i) update the health requirements on commercial imports of dogs, cats and ferrets to take account of the **Community Regulation (regulations 2(2)(a) and 2(3))**;

(ii) exempt animals which have entered a British Isles jurisdiction (other than Scotland or Wales) in accordance with the Community Regulation and rules equivalent to the **Non Commercial Movement Regulations** from the requirements of the principal Order on entry to England **(regulation 2(2)(b))**;

(iii) exempt animals which enter England in accordance with the Community Regulation and the **Non Commercial Movement Regulations** from the requirements of the principal Order **(regulation 2(4)**;

(iv) update the provisions allowing for early release from quarantine to take account of the **Community Regulation (regulation 2(6))**; and

(v) update the requirement to vaccinate animals in quarantine to take account of the **Community Regulation (regulation 2(7))**.

Ok, did you get that?

To translate it means that if you bring your pet dog home from abroad he needs an up-to-date pet passport to avoid quarantine for six months. It's just a series of injections and a couple of blood tests. Usually it's quite easy if you follow the instructions of your vet before you leave. The **Non Commercial Movement of Pet Animals (England) Regulations 2004** is a statutory instrument (S.I) as opposed to an **Act of Parliament** but still has the same authority.

Yes, it's that simple! But make sure you do things in plenty of time.

Our first date. Very romantic!

Conclusion

- You require a license to breed, sell, board or quarantine dogs.

- It is an offence to sell a puppy under 8 weeks old.
- You must keep accurate records of the animals in your care.
- Failure to comply with the rules may mean a loss of your licence.
- Breaches of the law can result in fines, imprisonment or both.
- Have your pet microchipped

- Have your pet vaccinated
- Arrange a blood test (Your vet will advise you as to when the tests are required.)

- Get PETS documentation

- Before your pet enters the UK, it must be treated against ticks and a tapeworm

- Your pet must be treated against ticks and tapeworms not less than 24 hours and not more than 48 hours before it is checked in with an approved transport company for its journey into the UK.

- Arrange for your animal to travel with an approved transport company on an authorised route

- *Your dog or cat may not enter the UK under PETS until six calendar months have passed from the date that your vet took the blood sample which led to a satisfactory test result.*

- *Once the vet has issued the PETS documentation and that six month period has passed, the PETS documentation is valid for your pet to enter the UK[1].*

- A list of countires elegible to issue passports is available from the DeFRA website. (See "Useful Addresses" section)

---

[1] Italicised text, crown copyright applies.

Useful addresses

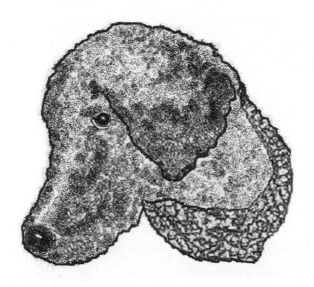

Companion Animal Welfare Council

CAWC Secretariat
The Dene
Old North Road
Bourn
Cambridge
CB23 2TZ
Tel/Fax 01954 718882
Email: cawc@cawc.freeserve.co.uk

<u>The Law Society</u> <u>**London**</u>

The Law Society's Hall
113 Chancery Lane
London WC2A 1PL
General enquiries line
+44 (0) 20 7242 1222

<u>Royal College of Veterinary Surgeons</u>

Belgravia House
62-64 Horseferry Road
London SW1P 2AF

Tel: (020) 7222 2001
Fax: (020) 7222 2004
Email: admin@rcvs.org.uk

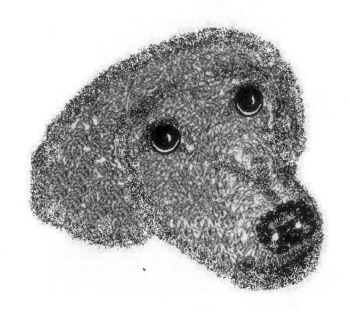

<u>RSPCA</u>

RSPCA Enquiries Service,
Wilberforce Way,
Southwater,
Horsham,
West Sussex RH13 9RS
www.rspca.org.uk
Cruelty line: 0300 1234 999
Advice line: 0300 1234 555
Donation line: 0300 123 0346